NORTH AMERICAN INDIAN
BEADWORK PATTERNS

NORTH AMERICAN INDIAN BEADWORK PATTERNS

PAMELA STANLEY-MILLNER

DOVER PUBLICATIONS, INC.
New York

GREEN EDITION ®

At Dover Publications we're committed to producing books in an earth-friendly manner and to helping our customers make greener choices.

Manufacturing books in the United States ensures compliance with strict environmental laws and eliminates the need for international freight shipping, a major contributor to global air pollution. And printing on recycled paper helps minimize our consumption of trees, water and fossil fuels.

The text of this book was printed on paper made with 50% post-consumer waste and the cover was printed on paper made with 10% post-consumer waste. At Dover, we use Environmental Paper Network's Paper Calculator to measure the benefits of these choices, including: the number of trees saved, gallons of water conserved, as well as air emissions and solid waste eliminated.

Courier Corporation, the manufacturer of this book, owns the Green Edition Trademark.

Please visit the product page for *North American Indian Beadwork Patterns* at www.doverpublications.com to see a detailed account of the environmental savings we've achieved over the life of this book.

In appreciation for their support, this book is dedicated, with love, to my husband James and my children Clinton John, Matthew Aaron and Cassandra Esther. I also want to pay tribute to my parents, Robert and Lois Stanley, and my mother-in-law Syril and father-in-law Norton Millner, who is celebrating his 70th birthday this year.

Bibliographical Note

North American Indian Beadwork Patterns is a new work, first published by Dover Publications, Inc., in 1995.

Library of Congress Cataloging-in-Publication Data

Stanley-Millner, Pamela.
    North American Indian beadwork patterns / Pamela Stanley-Millner.
        p.   cm.
    ISBN 0-486-28835-8 (pbk.)
    1. Indian beadwork—North America—Patterns.   I. Title.
E98.B46S73   1995
745.58'2—dc20   95–23623
                                                                                        CIP

Manufactured in the United States by Courier Corporation
28835810
www.doverpublications.com

Introduction

American Indian beadwork is on display in many museums around the country. Its splendid colors and vibrant patterns enlivening belts, dresses, headbands and other leather artifacts are a testament to the skill of many hands and the eye for beauty of many tribes. In the pages that follow, you will find complete instructions for two types of traditional American Indian bead application—bead weaving and appliqué beading—plus 85 authentic American Indian beadwork designs, 73 charted on graph paper for bead weaving and 12 drawn as full-size patterns for appliqué. You will find it possible to achieve the very striking effects you have admired and will be surprised to discover how simple the techniques are.

Beadcraft has such a long history in American Indian culture that the origin of many designs is obscure. Some bead designs are representational. For example, a cross symbolizes the four winds; a zigzag line, lightning. Characteristic designs differentiate the beadwork of one tribe from that of another. Some favor geometrics; others, florals; still others, animal depictions. Tribal origin is specified for each beadwork design included in this book. You will be able to see for yourself which tribes favor which motifs.

BEADS. In Columbus's day, coastal American Indians used shells, both in their natural state and shaped and polished into wampum, as the beads for their fancy work. Not long, however, after the arrival of the European settlers, French traders bartering with the Indians for furs introduced glass beads from Italy. These first glass beads, called pony beads, were eagerly adopted and soon incorporated in Indian beadwork and eventually replaced shell beads.

Pony beads were larger—five times larger—than the beads commonly in use today. The Indians fashioned them, despite their size, into elaborate necklaces and beaded patterns on fringed shirts and dresses. Pony beads have not disappeared, but the small glass seed bead—an import from Czechoslovakia—became popular around 1850 and remains the favorite to this day.

Both opaque and transparent seed beads are readily available in many different colors. They also come in various circumferences ranging from the largest, size 10 (10°), to smallest, size 14 (14°). Size 12 beads are the most versatile: they can be used for both bead weaving and appliqué beading, the two techniques covered in this book. Almost all projects shown in color on the covers are worked with size 12 beads.

THREAD. The original thread for beadwork came from sinew, the tough, fibrous, connective tissue of animals. The American Indian split the sinew from deer and buffalo into strands fine enough for stringing beads; the prepared sinew is still available—but something of a novelty—even today. When cotton threads became commercially available in the 1800s, they easily gained acceptance in beadwork. More recently they have been joined by nylon.

Cotton crochet thread No. 30 is recommended for warping the loom in bead weaving; it is readily available in needlework shops and at notion counters. Nylon thread Size 0, combining the virtues of strength and fineness, is ideal for the threaded needlework in both bead weaving and bead appliqué; it is available in stores carrying supplies for beading.

It is recommended, in both bead weaving and bead appliqué, to thread the needle in two-foot lengths at a time. In bead weaving this two-foot length is single strand; in bead appliqué, both two-foot lengths are double strand.

WAX. Whether using cotton or nylon thread in the needle, wax it to prevent tangles or breakage. A fine residual wax coat is all that's necessary to hold the thread fibers in place. Beeswax sold in cakes at sewing notion counters is excellent. Wax the full length of thread you'll be working with, first on one side and then on the other.

The *warp* threads in bead weaving do not need waxing: they are a three-stranded thread and therefore very unlikely to break, and they are held taut during the beading and cannot tangle.

NEEDLES. A needle specially designed for the purpose—a beading needle—is used in both bead weaving and bead appliqué to pick up the beads in pattern order. Longer and thinner than the average sewing needle, the beading needle will minimize broken beads and frayed threads. Averaging two inches in length, beading needles are available in Nos. 10 through 16—the higher the number, the thinner the needle. No. 16 is recommended and is available from craft suppliers.

The *second* needle in appliqué beading must easily penetrate the material on which the design will be appliquéd (for example, garment leather or velvet). A No. 9 sharp, commonly available for hand sewing, is recommended.

MAIL ORDER SUPPLIES. If the materials you need for beadwork are not available from local suppliers, the following trading post will be able to help you by mail:

Western Trading Post
P.O. Box 9070
Denver, CO 80209-0070

Bead Weaving

Loom Construction. The most important tool for bead weaving is a loom. Generally speaking, you can build a loom longer and wider than any you can buy. Greater loom length and width translates into larger bead weavings. Besides, constructing a loom is *easy*. The necessary wood, along with nails and screws, is readily available from a hardware store or lumberyard; it may even turn up among odds and ends you have at home. You will need the following wood and hardware: one 36″ × 7″ × ¾″ board (base of the loom);* two 11″ × 7″ × ¾″ boards (sides of the loom); 8 wood screws, 1½″ long; 2 medium-sized nails, ¾″ long.

Fasten the sides to the base with the screws (see *Fig. 1*). Space the screws evenly, four at each end, and tighten them securely.

Figure 1: Bead Loom

This is crucial to the stability of the loom. Next, pound the nails into the side boards, one nail exactly in the center of each board on the outside. Leave the nails protruding ¼″ (see *Fig. 1*). The nails are essential for warping the loom. Last, the tops of the sides must be notched with very narrow incisions as illustrated in *Fig. 2*. Starting ⅜″ from one end and using a

Figure 2: Detail of Notches along Top of Side

sharp knife, make the notches 1/16″ deep and 1/16″ apart. Use a ruler as a placement guide. Cut approximately 100 notches in the top of each side, leaving a ⅜″ margin at each end. These notches will space the warp threads and hold them in position.

The Warp Count. Before you warp the loom, refer to the charted design from which you are planning to work. Each vertical line equals one warp thread. Check for the number of warp threads the design requires. For your convenience, this count is given under every bead-weaving chart in this volume. The warp count is always *one more* than the total number of beads across one horizontal row of the design.

To center the warp threads on the loom, divide the warp count in half. Then, along *both* sides of the loom, count that

halved number of notches *from* the center toward either end; be sure to count in the same direction on both sides. Mark these parallel notches temporarily with a small piece of tape.

Warping the Loom. To begin warping the loom, tie the end of the cotton crochet thread No. 30 to the nail on one side of the loom (see *Fig. 2*). Next, bring the thread up this same side and into the notch you have marked. Holding the thread in the notch with a finger, extend the thread the length of the loom to the parallel notch you have marked on the other side. Pull the warp thread taut and secure it in position by wrapping it around the nail in this side (see *Fig. 1*). Continue in this manner, warping first in one direction and then in the other, always through the next set of parallel notches, wrapping around one nail and the other in turn, until you have the total number of warp threads necessary for the design. Again, as at the beginning, tie off the thread on a nail and cut.

The Charts. In all 73 charts for bead weaving, each square on the chart equals one bead. As you weave, read the charts in horizontal rows from top to bottom, returning to the top of the chart for the repeat unless otherwise indicated. Read each row from left to right.

Each chart is accompanied by a key to the bead color represented by each symbol. The unmarked squares—the background—are beaded in white unless another color is specified.

Technique. Thread the No. 16 beading needle with a two-foot single strand of Size 0 nylon thread (Remember to wax it). Hold the warped loom across your lap, extending to the left and right, or support it on a table. A couple of inches from the left notches, tie the loose end of the nylon thread to the warp thread closest to you. Then, reading from left to right across the top row of the design chart, pick up, in order, with the point of the threaded needle, the number and color of beads needed to complete the first row of the design. Slide the beads down the nylon thread to the knot.

Next, pass the needle and thread carrying the strung beads *under* the warp threads from left to right (away from you) and hold the needle in back (on the right) so that the thread with the beads is fairly taut underneath the warp. With the index finger of your free hand, push up each bead in turn, from left to right (front to back), between a pair of warp threads. Eventually your index finger will be holding the entire row of beads in place.

The return of the threaded needle through the beads *above* the warp threads will secure the row. Work from right to left (back to front) in four- or five-bead sections until the entire row of beads is threaded above the warp threads as well as below (see *Fig. 3*). Then return to the chart for the second row, third and so on. Each row is worked the same way.

Figure 3: Bead Weaving

*A common bead weaving is the belt. If you plan to fit waist sizes larger than 36 inches, make your loom with a longer base; or else plan to adjust the fit by extending the leather backing of the bead weaving.

The thread in your needle will not last forever. If you don't have enough to pass *both* under *and* over the warp to secure an entire row of beads, go back one row and run the needle and thread *from* the outside edge through a half dozen or so beads. No knot is necessary; the tucked thread will hold. Cut off any loose end remaining. Then rethread the needle, wax the thread, but don't tie it to the warp. Instead, in the last row worked, run the needle and thread through a half dozen or so beads *to* the outside edge, securing the end in this way without a knot. Proceed to reading the next row of the chart and picking up the necessary beads in order.

Fit and Sizing. The many belts shown on the covers fulfill two essentials of strong impact: the design repetitions are not only complete, but also symmetrically spaced along the total length. The ends join visually as well as functionally, as is necessary in a belt. When both fit and look are critical, plan ahead by checking the gauge—the number of beads to the horizontal inch and the number of rows to the vertical inch— and using it to your advantage.

Let's assume you wish to make a belt to fit a 25½" waist and are not concerned about width. On the design chart you plan to use, the count of horizontal rows from the beginning to the end of one complete design is 25. By weaving a small sample with the beads you plan to use, you discover that there are 5 rows of beads to the inch. Dividing 25 by 5 yields the design length: 5". Allowing ½" of waist size for securing the belt ends together, your bead weaving 25" long could conceivably consist of 5 design repetitions; but there would then be no space whatsoever in between. Four repetitions, however, would leave background space, 5" altogether that would distribute evenly in 1" units, 5 rows of background beads each. The choice is yours *before* the commitment of time and effort.

In many design charts, background can be added and subtracted as fit requires. In the designs that run continuously, if you cannot adjust size by adding or subtracting a design repetition, you may need to switch to another size bead. Of course, you can always *add* length by means of the leather or other material used in the finishing of your bead weaving.

Binding Off and Finishing. 1" masking tape is very handy for binding off a bead-weaving project at each end. While the completed piece is still on the taut warp threads of the loom, run the tape above and below the warp threads next to the first and last rows of beads. Press the tape-warp-tape sandwiches together; the warp threads, permanently secured against unraveling, can then be cut, leaving the masking tape seals at either end of your bead weaving. Fold the masking tape to the back of the design and stitch it down.

After masking tape is used to bind off, whip-stitch the bead weaving by hand to a strip of garment leather or other material longer than the beaded piece. The extending ends of backing become the ties for a belt or the mounting of a wall hanging. This style of finishing is very common, and a number of examples appear on the covers.

Binding off can also be accomplished, in part or altogether, by tapering the ends of a bead weaving through decreases. An example is shown on the cover. Beginning a project with increases is difficult and fortunately unnecessary: leave enough room on the warp threads at the beginning of the project to go back and decrease *after* having completed the rest of the piece. Leave space for as many rows as the number of beads to be decreased.

Let's assume you are working background rows and wish to decrease from 12 beads to 6. Pick up 10 beads for the next row, and double up warp threads between the first and the last two beads. Work another row 10 beads wide. Continue in this manner, decreasing 2 beads per row every other row—two rows of 8, two rows of 6—until the tapering is complete.

If the bead weaving will be backed, proceed with binding off and finishing as above, with the possible addition of an overhand knot where the ties begin. If the bead weaving will not be backed, cut the warp threads, leaving ends long enough to tie in an overhand knot and/or tuck back into previous rows of beads.

Appliqué Beading

Once you choose a design for bead appliqué, place tracing paper over the full-size pattern in the book, secure it with paper clips and copy in pen or pencil. Don't copy the color key numbers in the pattern; it's easier to refer to them in the book as you work.

It's also necessary to choose the material on which to bead appliqué. Suede, garment leather and velvet are all suitable for bead appliqué; the project—purse, vest, wall hanging—will determine what's best. Keep in mind whether the bead colors in the pattern will stand out on the color background you choose. If the background material must be a given color, you may wish to adjust bead colors for a stronger effect.

Once you have a pattern tracing and material to work on, you're ready to transfer the pattern from the tracing to the material. Work on a piece of material *larger* than the finished dimensions of the project; cut to size *after* the appliqué beading is complete. Place the material right side up on a flat surface. Next, place a sheet of carbon paper—larger than the pattern— on the material, carbon side down, followed by the pattern tracing, tracing side up. Holding all three layers securely in position, firmly retrace the entire pattern with pen or pencil; the pressure should transfer a carbon outline of the pattern to the material for bead appliqué. No special carbon paper is required; you may use dressmaker's carbon if you prefer, especially if you need a *light* outline on a *dark* material.

Once the design is transferred and the material is ready for appliqué, stretch it taut in an embroidery hoop or stapled to a frame. Use the color key accompanying the pattern in the book as a guide to the bead colors you will need. Once you have gathered together Size 0 nylon thread, a No. 16 beading needle, a No. 9 sharp needle, scissors and beeswax, you are ready to begin.

In beading all design elements, outline first, then fill in the interiors. Whether to outline with one, two or three rows of beads is determined by overall design proportions. Bead the interiors along lines that enhance the look of a given motif.

Thread each needle with a double strand of nylon thread two feet long, ends knotted together. Remember to wax it. Begin with the beading needle. Draw it from the back to the front of the stretched material, and pull until the knot is tight against the back. Do this at a point in the pattern where it is logical to begin laying down beads to outline a design element (for example, a leaf, a petal, a bud). Then string enough beads on the thread to cover the outline of this design element, but not so many that there won't be a loose end of thread with which to tie off.

Now take up the other needle, the No. 9 sharp. If you are right-handed, work this needle with your right hand; if left-handed, favor this needle with your left. Bring the sharp up from the back of the material in the same manner as the beading needle, but positioned to tack the bead-carrying thread to the design outline between the first and second beads. Proceed accordingly: go back through the material, completing the tacking of the first thread with the second thread between the first and second beads (see *Fig. 4*). The appliqué of the first bead is complete.

The remaining beads are secured in the same fashion but in intervals of three or four beads between tacks. Just be sure to

Figure 4: Bead Appliqué

needle & thread holding beads

needle & thread securing beads

tack frequently enough that the beads hold the outline of the design. Follow this procedure throughout the appliqué project, even for filling in the interiors of the design.

When either thread is running out, pull it through to the wrong side of the material and knot, either by chain stitching or by tying to other threads on the wrong side. *Don't knot to the material:* this would show on the right side. Rethread your needle, wax the thread and continue, checking the color key of the pattern for what beads to use next.

Once the bead appliqué is complete, release the material from the embroidery hoop or stretcher frame, cut to the necessary dimension for your project and hand or machine sew the finished piece.

The Designs

All designs rendered for bead weaving and appliqué beading were copied from American Indian artifacts found in museum collections in the United States. The following museums graciously consented to the inclusion of the designs on the following pages:

Department of Library Services, American Museum of Natural History, New York, New York: 7, 8, 26–27, 37 (Seminole), 38, 41, 43–55, 60.

Museum of the American Indian, Heye Foundation, New York, New York: 11, 12, 16, 17, 18 (New England tribe), 19, 20 (Winnebago), 21 (Winnebago), 22, 23, 24 (Plains Cree), 25 (Arapaho), 30, 31 (Cheyenne), 33, 34 (Crow), 36, 39, 40 (Klamath).

New Jersey State Museum, Trenton: 20–21 (Delaware), 35 (Sioux), 42, 63, 64.

Milwaukee Public Museum, Wisconsin: 13, 18 (Sioux), 31 (Woodland).

Department of Anthropology, Smithsonian Institution, Washington, D.C.: 14, 15, 28, 29, 37 (Kiowa).

Field Museum of Natural History, Chicago, Illinois: 24–25 (Washo), 32, 40 (Flathead), 56, 58, 59, 62.

The Montclair Art Museum, New Jersey: 34 (Sioux), 40 (Arapaho), 57, 61.

Charts for Bead Weaving

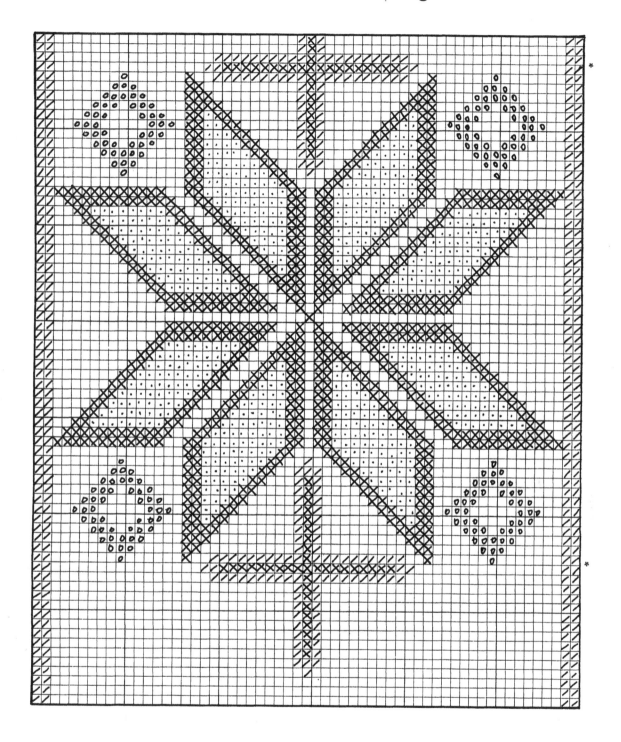

WINNEBAGO

60 warp threads

COLOR KEY   ⊘ navy blue

⊡ yellow

⊠ red

⊙ green

white background

Repeat from * to * for pattern.

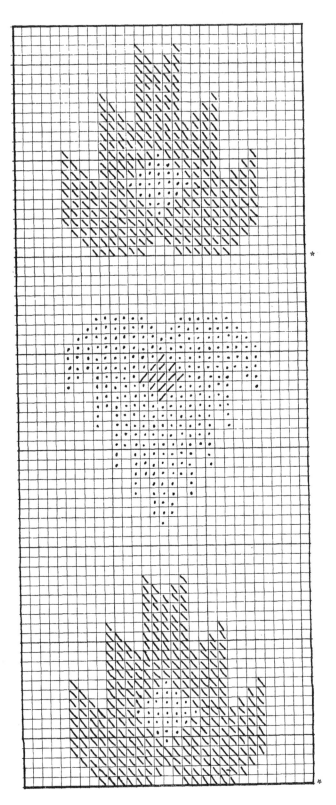

PLAINS CREE

23 warp threads

COLOR KEY ⊘ yellow
            ⊡ black
            ⊙ white
            ⊠ medium blue
                white background

MENOMINEE

32 warp threads

COLOR KEY ⊡ mustard
            ⧅ medium blue
                white background

Repeat from * to * for pattern.

CHEYENNE

16 warp threads

COLOR KEY · red

light blue background

ALGONQUIAN

42 warp threads

COLOR KEY ⊘ yellow

· red

blue background

Repeat from * to * for pattern.

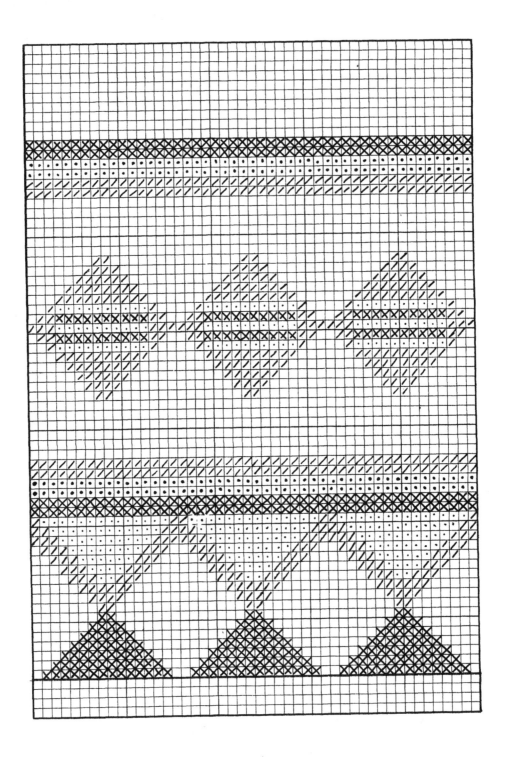

PLAINS

49 warp threads

COLOR KEY ☑ red

☒ navy blue

◉ light blue

⊡ white

medium green background

SOUTHERN PLAINS

30 warp threads

COLOR KEY   ⊠   red

                ⊙   yellow

                ⧄   navy blue

                ⊡   light blue

                    white background

Repeat from * to * for pattern.

CADDOAN VILLAGERS

36 warp threads

COLOR KEY   ⊡   black

                    white background

                    warp threads: 11 red

                               8 white

                               9 red

                               5 white

                               5 red

Repeat from * to * for pattern.

WINNEBAGO

82 warp threads

COLOR KEY ☑ dark blue
             ☒ green
             ◉ yellow
             ⊡ orange
               white background

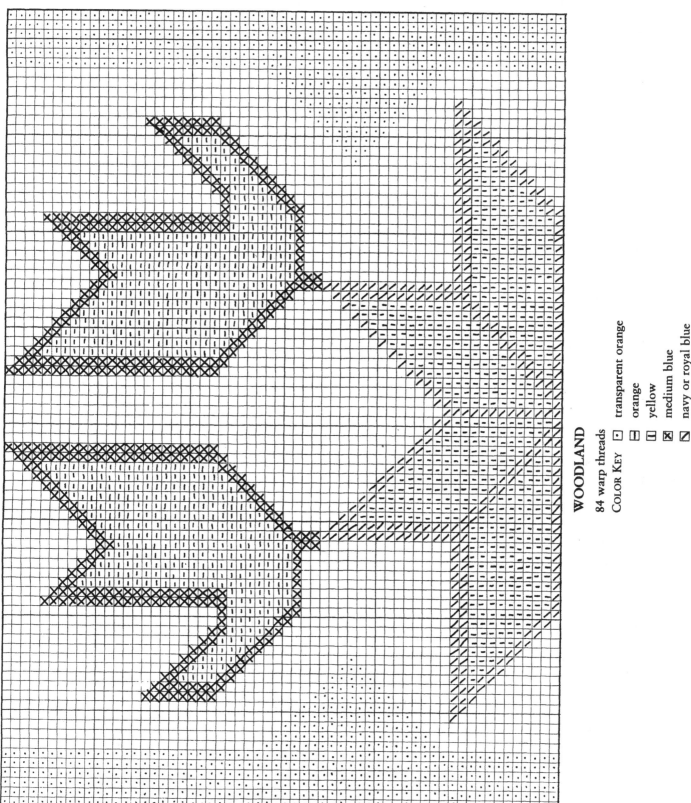

WOODLAND

84 warp threads

COLOR KEY ⊡ transparent orange

⊞ orange

Ⅱ yellow

☒ medium blue

◩ navy or royal blue

KIOWA

60 warp threads

COLOR KEY ⊘ navy blue
 ⊡ black
 ⊠ mustard yellow
 white background

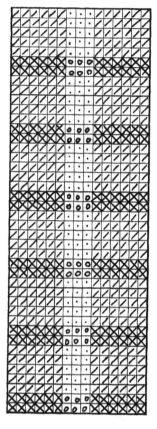

ARAPAHO

16 warp threads

COLOR KEY   ◺   green

                   ⊡   red

                   ⊠   yellow

                   ◉   navy blue

SEMINOLE

32 warp threads

COLOR KEY   ◿   black

                   ◙   medium blue

                   ⊡   wine red

                   ◉   dark green

                   ⊠   yellow

                   ◤   navy blue

                   Ⅱ   dark yellow

Work from A to C, then from C back to B. Continue working from B to C to B for desired length.

15

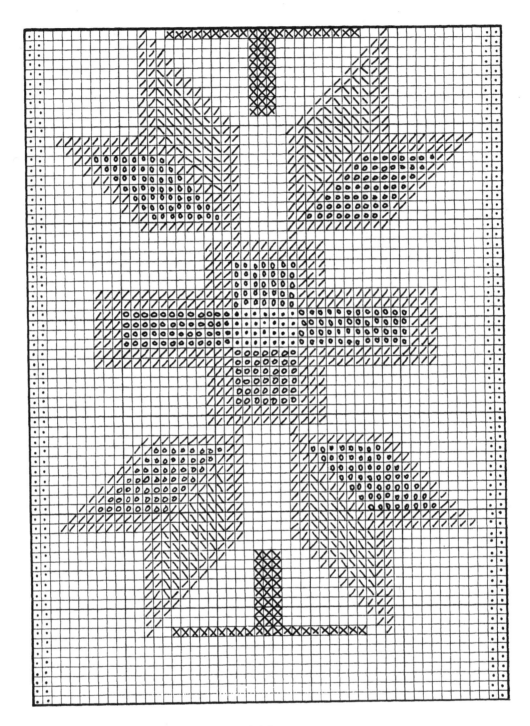

WINNEBAGO

52 warp threads

COLOR KEY ⊠ dark green
           ⊙ red
           ◩ black
           ⊡ medium blue
           ◙ yellow
           ◩ light blue

PAIUTE

24 warp threads

COLOR KEY · red

⧄ navy blue

⧅ medium yellow

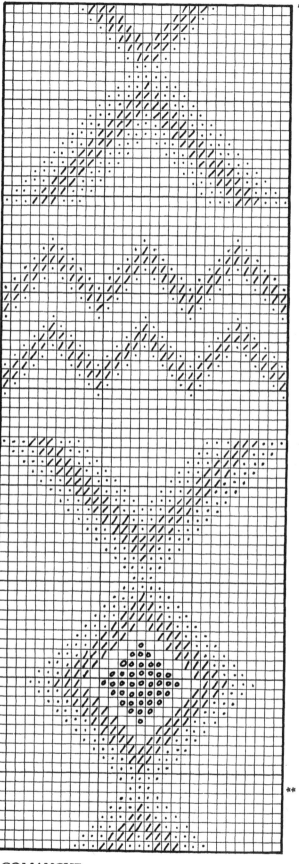

COMANCHE

32 warp threads

COLOR KEY · white

⧄ red

blue background

Work from * to **, then from ** back to * for pattern.   17

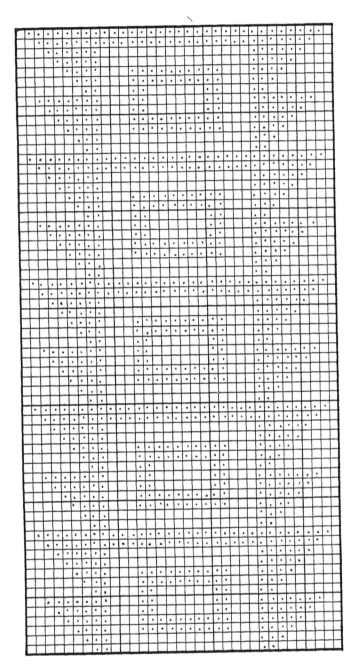

NEW ENGLAND TRIBE

35 warp threads

COLOR KEY ⊡ white
black background
warp threads: red

SIOUX

19 warp threads

COLOR KEY ◪ red
⊡ medium blue
⊠ navy blue
⊞ yellow

KICKAPOO
Shown in color on back cover.

48 warp threads

COLOR KEY   ⊠   white
                ⊠   medium blue
                ⊡   pink
                    black background

Repeat from A to C for pattern; end last repeat at B.

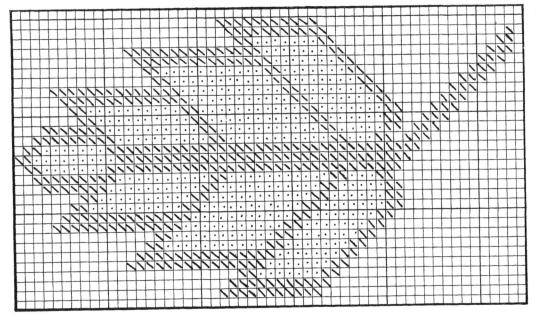

WINNEBAGO

32 warp threads

COLOR KEY

☑ black

⊡ medium green

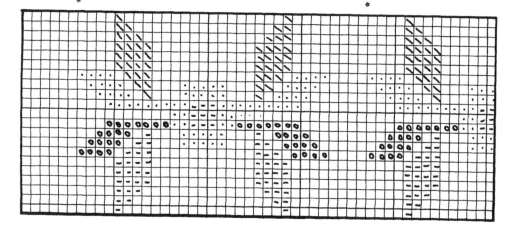

WINNEBAGO

22 warp threads

COLOR KEY   ◙   red
              ⊡   medium blue
              ⊠   green
              ⊞   yellow

Repeat from * to * for pattern.

DELAWARE

Shown in color on back cover.

46 warp threads

COLOR KEY   ⊠   light blue
              ⊡   red

              warp threads: red

Work from A to C; repeat from B to C as desired, then work from C to D.

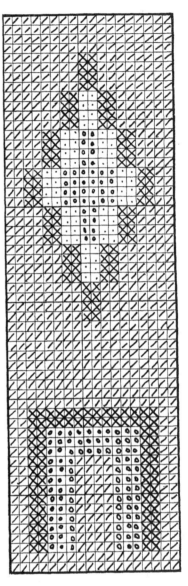

SARCEE

19 warp threads

COLOR KEY ☒ medium blue

         ⊡ red

         ◪ medium green

         ⊡ yellow

SAUK & FOX

46 warp threads

COLOR KEY ⊡ red

         ☒ black

         ◨ medium blue

         ◪ yellow

KICKAPOO ▶

62 warp threads

COLOR KEY ⊡ orange

         ◪ yellow

         ◉ navy blue

         ⊟ red

         ☒ light blue

           navy blue background

Repeat from * to * for pattern.

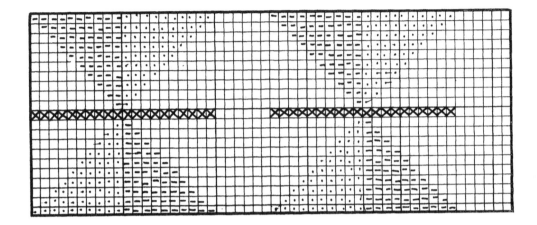

ARAPAHO

22 warp threads

COLOR KEY   ⊞ red

         ⊡ green

         ⊠ navy blue

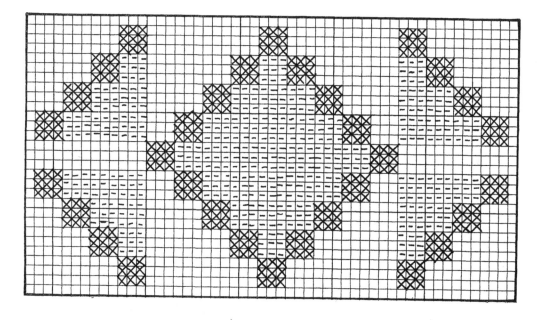

PLAINS CREE

30 warp threads

COLOR KEY ⊠ navy blue
           Ⅱ red
           ⊞ light blue background

B

C

D

WASHO

Shown in color on front cover.

52 warp threads

COLOR KEY ☑ black
           ⊠ medium blue
           ⊡ orange
           Ⅱ yellow
           ⊙ red
           ⊞ light blue

Work from A to D, repeating B to C as desired; then work from D back to A.

25

SAUK & FOX
Shown in color on front and back covers.

64 warp threads

COLOR KEY

⊞	black
·	light blue
⧄	red
⊙	pink
⊠	light brown
⧄	navy blue
⧄	medium green

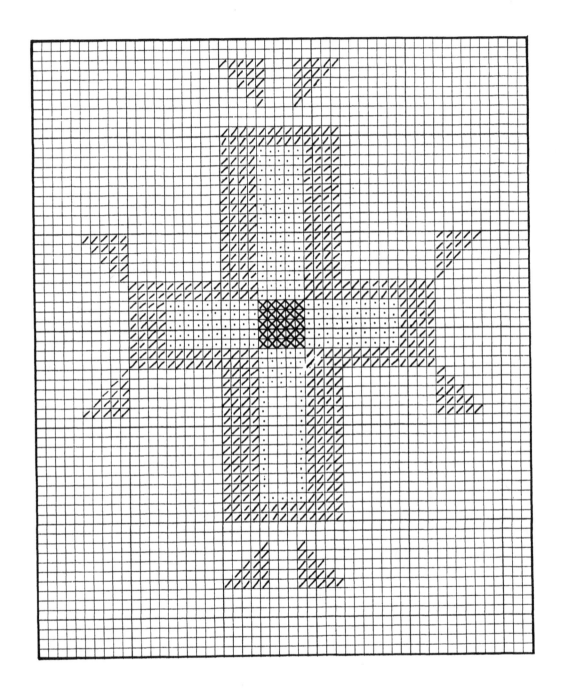

SIOUX

54 warp threads

COLOR KEY ⧄ yellow

⊡ red

⊠ royal blue

royal blue background

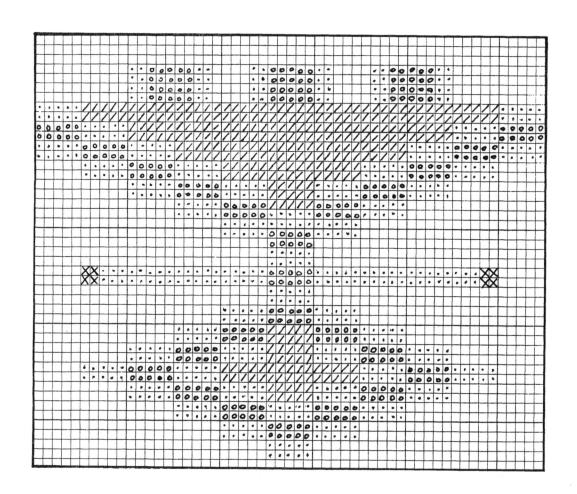

BLACKFOOT

56 warp threads

COLOR KEY ☑ orange

⊡ royal blue

◙ pink

SAUK & FOX
Shown in color on back cover.

38 warp threads

COLOR KEY   ⊡ pink
                ◢ blue
                ◿ dark blue
                ⊙ red
                ⊠ black
                ⊡ yellow

PAIUTE
Shown in color on front cover.

24 warp threads

COLOR KEY   ◿ medium blue
                ⊠ red
                ⊙ medium yellow

CHEYENNE

35 warp threads

COLOR KEY   ◉   medium blue

          ⊠   navy blue

          ⊞   yellow

          ◨   red

          ⊡   green

             light blue background

WOODLAND

14 warp threads

COLOR KEY   ⟋   royal blue

          ⊡   red

          ⊟   green

          ◉   yellow

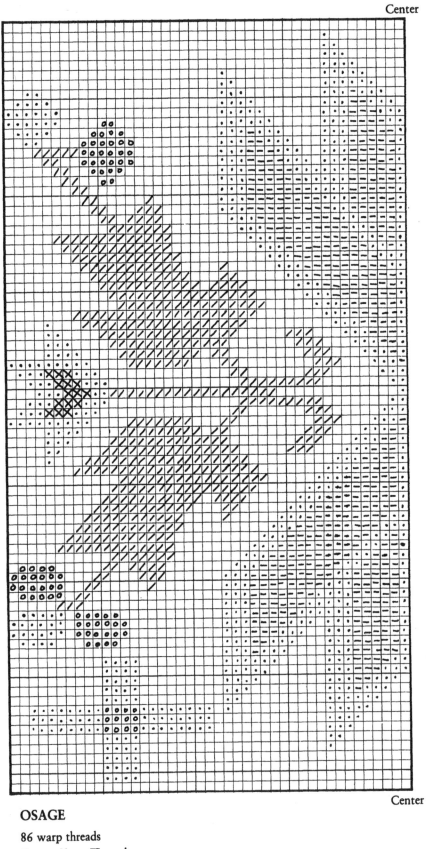

Center

OSAGE

86 warp threads

COLOR KEY 　⦿　red

　　　　　　▧　green

　　　　　　⊡　blue

　　　　　　⊟　light blue

　　　　　　⊠　pink

This is one half of the total design. Reverse pattern vertically for next repeat.

WINNEBAGO

Shown in color on front cover.

68 warp threads

COLOR KEY ◙ red

⬊ blue

⊡ light green

⬕ navy blue

33

Work from A to C, then from C back to B. Continue to work from B to C to B for desired length.

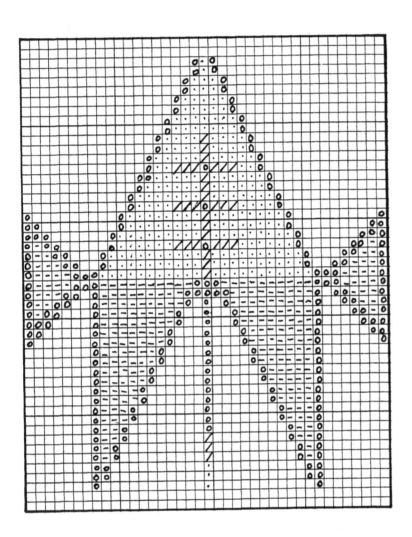

CROW

40 warp threads

COLOR KEY ⊡ red

⊡ navy blue

⊘ yellow

⊟ green

SIOUX

14 warp threads

COLOR KEY ⊘ red

⊡ green

⊠ navy blue

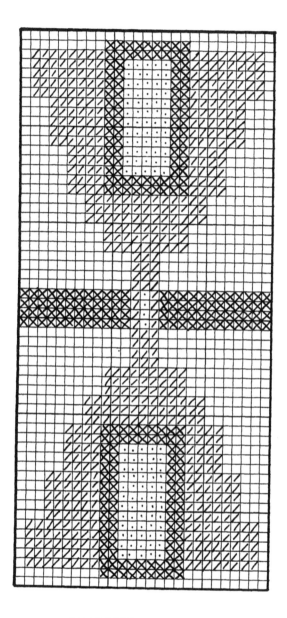

ARAPAHO

28 warp threads

COLOR KEY ▨ dark green
           ⊠ red
           ⊡ light blue

SIOUX

22 warp threads

COLOR KEY ▨ red
           ⊡ green
           ⊡ dark blue

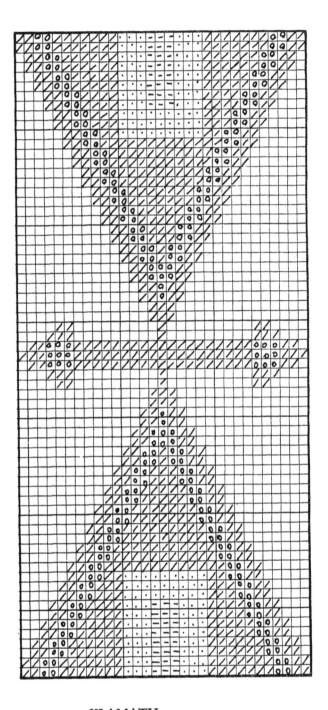

ASSINIBOIN

25 warp threads

COLOR KEY   ☒   medium blue

                 ⊡   green

KLAMATH

32 warp threads

COLOR KEY   ☑   medium blue

                 ⊡   white

                 ⊟   green

                 ◙   mustard yellow

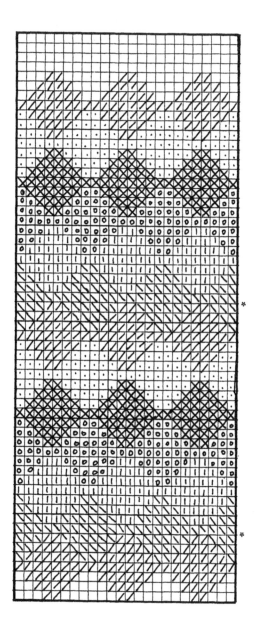

KIOWA

22 warp threads

COLOR KEY ☑ white

                ⊡ red

                  royal blue background

SEMINOLE

25 warp threads

COLOR KEY ☑ white

                ⊡ black

                ⊠ red

                ⊙ light blue

                ⊞ blue

                ◩ pink

Repeat from * to * for pattern.

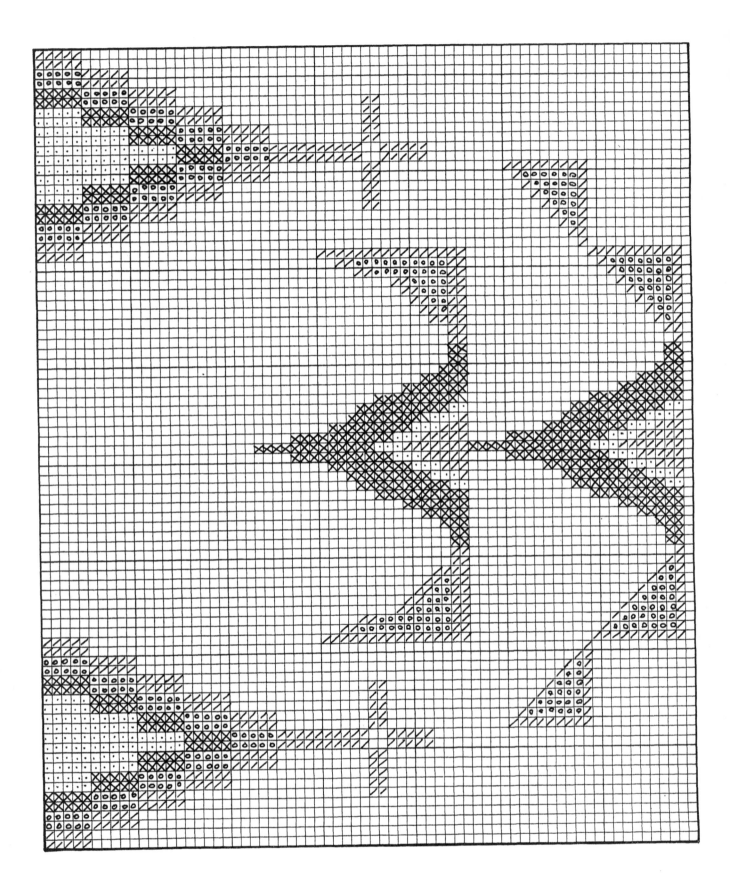

CROW ▲

Shown in color on front cover.

84 warp threads

COLOR KEY

  ◙ green
  ◿ red
  · yellow
  ⊠ navy blue

Reverse design for next repeat.

POTAWATOMI

66 warp threads

COLOR KEY

  ◙ gold
  ⊠ navy blue
  · light blue
  ◿ red

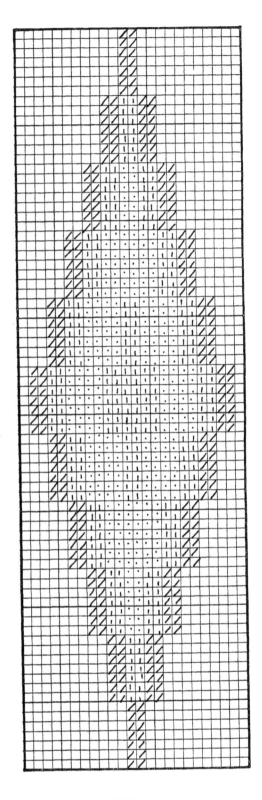

KLAMATH

28 warp threads

COLOR KEY   ⧄   red

            ⊡   navy blue

            ⊙   green

            ⊟   pink

Repeat from * to * for inner pattern; continue sawtooth border sequence independently.

FLATHEAD

25 warp threads

COLOR KEY   ⧄   blue

            ⊓   red

            ⊡   turquoise

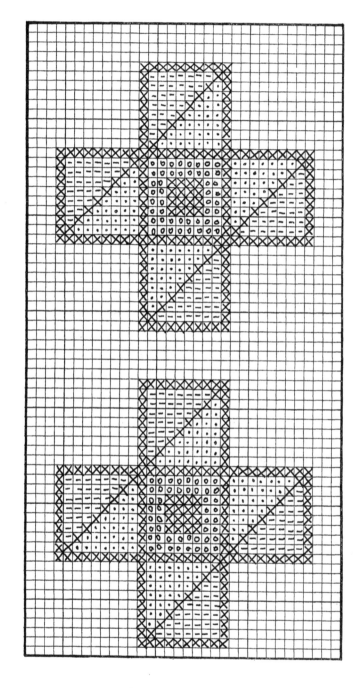

PLAINS CREE

22 warp threads

COLOR KEY   ⬚ green

            ◉ yellow

            ⧄ orange

DAKOTA SIOUX

35 warp threads

COLOR KEY   ⊡ red

            ◙ yellow

            ⊠ navy blue

            ⊟ green

CROW

44 warp threads

COLOR KEY ◙ yellow

⊡ green

⊟ navy blue

▨ red

CROW

21 warp threads

COLOR KEY ⊠ red

◙ yellow

⊡ green

⊟ navy blue

ARAPAHO

26 warp threads

COLOR KEY   ◩   red

◦   navy blue

◉   white

Repeat from * to * for pattern.

CHEYENNE

43 warp threads

COLOR KEY   ◉   navy blue

☒   green

⊡   white

◪   red

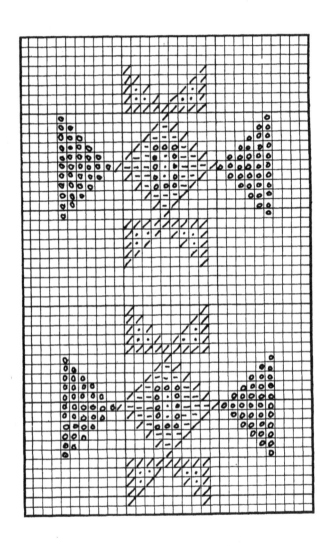

GROS VENTRE

30 warp threads

COLOR KEY   ⊡   yellow

            ⊠   navy blue

                 light blue background

DAKOTA SIOUX

32 warp threads

COLOR KEY   ⧄   red

            ⊡   yellow

            ⊡   navy blue

            ⊟   light blue

CHEYENNE

29 warp threads

COLOR KEY   ⧄   navy blue

            ⊙   red

            ⊡   green

SIOUX

29 warp threads

COLOR KEY   ⊡   red

            ⊠   navy blue

            ⊟   yellow

            ⊙   light blue

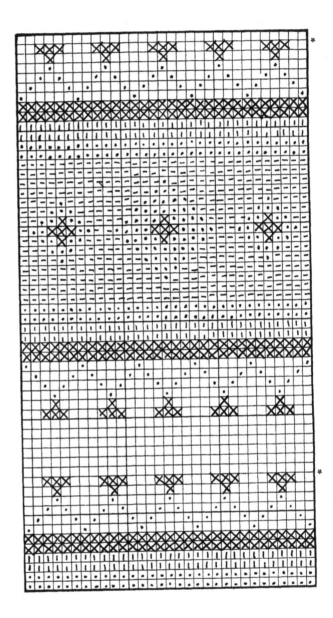

SIOUX

22 warp threads

COLOR KEY ☒ white
⊡ red
⊙ yellow
⊞ blue
light blue background

Repeat from * to * for pattern.

DAKOTA SIOUX

32 warp threads

COLOR KEY ☒ navy blue
⊡ red
⊞ yellow
⊟ light blue

Repeat from * to * for pattern.

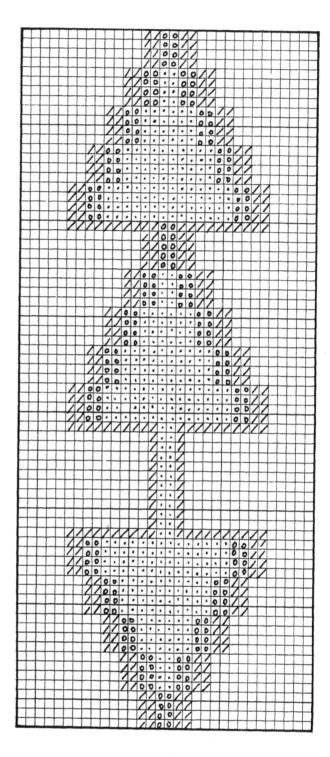

YAKIMA

20 warp threads

COLOR KEY   ⧄   red

             ⊞   blue

             ⊡   pink

Repeat from * to * for pattern.

YAKIMA

33 warp threads

COLOR KEY   ⧄   blue

             ◎   red

             ⊡   green

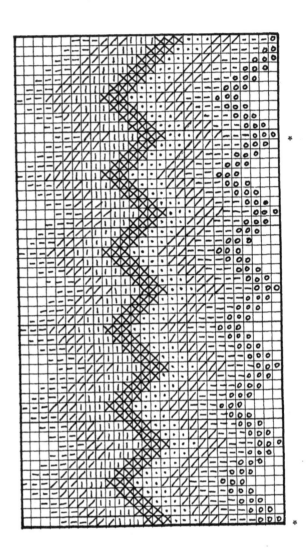

WINNEBAGO

27 warp threads

COLOR KEY
- ⊠ white
- ⊟ red
- ⊡ black
- ⊙ blue
- ◺ mustard

Repeat from * to * for pattern.

WINNEBAGO

29 warp threads

COLOR KEY
- ⊡ white
- ◙ pink
- ⊟ blue
- ◹ red
- ⊠ black
- ⥿ mustard

Repeat from * to * for pattern.

ARAPAHO

30 warp threads

COLOR KEY
- 🔘 red
- ⧆ navy blue
- ⊡ light blue
- ⊟ yellow
- ⊠ green

Repeat from * to * for pattern.

CROW

36 warp threads

COLOR KEY
- 🔘 red
- ⧄ blue

WINNEBAGO

44 warp threads

COLOR KEY   ◪   red

           ⊟   pink

           ⊡   green

           ⊠   black

WINNEBAGO

18 warp threads

COLOR KEY   ◉   light blue

           ⊠   red

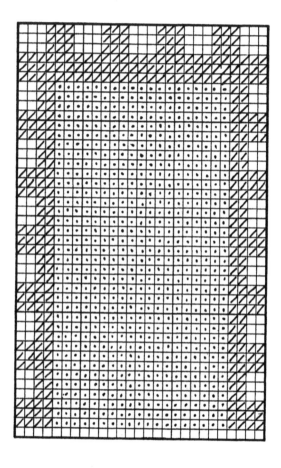

CROW

30 warp threads

COLOR KEY   ☑   navy blue

           ▣   red

           ⊡   green

CROW

28 warp threads

COLOR KEY   ☑   black

           ⊡   green

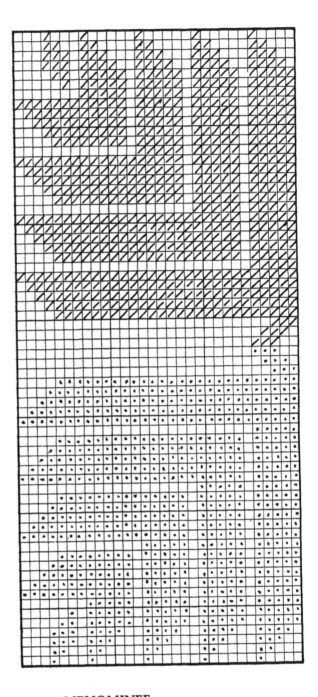

DAKOTA SIOUX

19 warp threads

COLOR KEY ▨ green
                ◉ navy blue
                ⊠ red

MENOMINEE

31 warp threads

COLOR KEY ⊡ red
                ▨ dark blue
                light blue background

Full-Size Patterns for Bead Appliqué

IROQUOIS

COLOR KEY 1-pink
2-yellow
3-light blue
4-red
5-light green

WINNEBAGO

Color Key   1-light blue
                         2-pink
                         3-red
                         4-blue
                         5-orange
                         6-green

WINNEBAGO

Color Key   1-medium blue
                      2-light blue
                      3-dark green
                      4-gold or yellow
                      5-red
                      6-turquoise

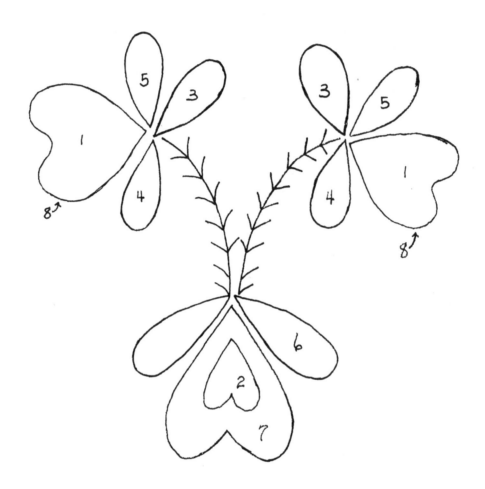

MENOMINEE

Color Key
1-green
2-gold
3-black
4-light blue
5-brown
6-dark blue
7-red
8-white
white stems

CHIPPEWA

COLOR KEY   1-gold
2-yellow
3-green
4-pink
5-red
6-white
7-light blue

POTAWATOMI

Color Key   1-light blue
2-dark red
3-light red
4-orange
5-white
6-dark green
7-light green

CREE

COLOR KEY   1-light green
2-dark green
3-red
4-pink
5-orange
6-brown
7-yellow
8-gray
9-white

PLAINS CREE

COLOR KEY
1-blue
2-wine red
3-red
4-pink
5-light green
6-dark green

CHIPPEWA

COLOR KEY
1-black
2-white
3-pink
4-red
5-blue
6-green
7-orange
8-light orange
9-dark blue

CHIPPEWA

COLOR KEY 1-light green
                2-dark green
                3-navy blue
                4-light blue
                5-yellow
                6-brown
                7-pink
                8-orange

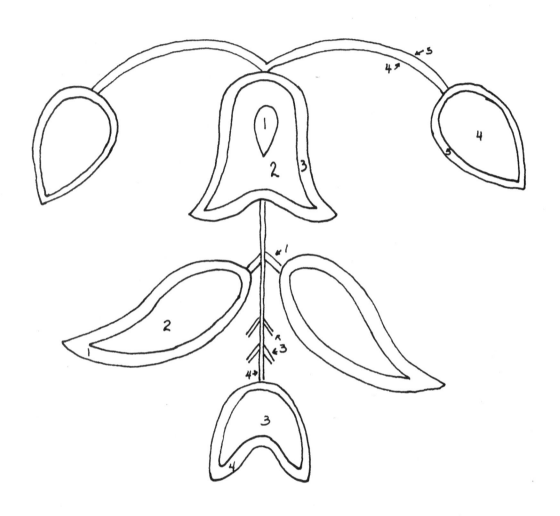

FLATHEAD

Color Key 1-red
2-yellow
3-light blue
4-navy blue
5-white

OJIBWA

COLOR KEY
1-navy blue
2-black
3-green
4-light blue
5-medium blue
6-pink
7-orange
8-yellow
9-dark pink